JOHN THOMPSON RECITAL SERIES

Intermediate to Advanced

THEME & VARIATIONS

5 GREAT ARRANGEMENTS BY JOHN THOMPSON

T0070926

ISBN 978-1-4803-9967-9

EXCLUSIVELY DISTRIBUTED BY

WILLIS MUSIC

HAL•LEONARD®
CORPORATION
7777 W. BLUEMOUND RD. P.O. BOX 13819
MILWAUKEE, WISCONSIN 53213

Visit Hal Leonard Online at
www.halleonard.com

Variations on
Three Blind Mice

Adapted by
John Thompson

THEME
Moderato con moto

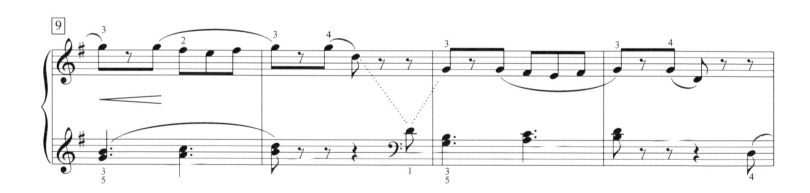

VAR. I

[The mice begin to scamper]

VAR. II

Espressivo

VAR. III
Con anima

VAR. IV
Andantino

Variations on
Mary Had a Little Lamb

Adapted by
John Thompson

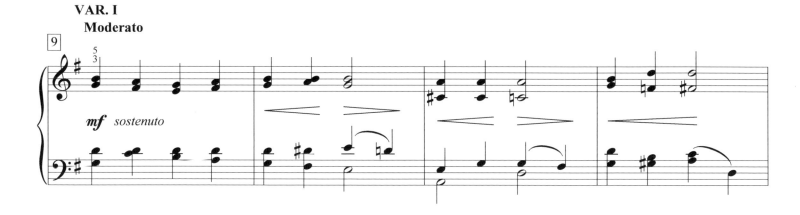

VAR. II

VAR. IV

Allegro scherzando

VAR. V

Allegro moderato

VAR. VI

Allegretto con brio

VAR. VIII
Tempo di valse

Variations on
Twinkle, Twinkle, Little Star

Adapted by
John Thompson

VAR. VI
Allegretto con brio

VAR. VII
Allegro non troppo

VAR. VIII
Tempo di valse

Variations on
Twinkle, Twinkle, Little Star

Adapted by
John Thompson

VAR. V (a la Hungarian Dance)
Allegro vivace ♩ = 120

Variations on
Chopsticks

Adapted by
John Thompson

VAR. V (a la Hungarian Dance)
Allegro vivace ♩ = 120

Variations on
Chopsticks

Adapted by
John Thompson

VAR. IV

Andante maestoso (March)

VAR. V
Tempo di Valser

VAR. IV

Andante maestoso (March)

VAR. VI
Moderato (Spanish Dance)

Dedicated to Jeanne Perron

Variations on
Chopin's C Minor Prelude
Op. 28, No. 20

Frederic Chopin
1810–1849
Adapted by John Thompson

VAR. I

Capriccioso ♩= c. 66

VAR. III (a la Mendelssohn)

VAR. IV (a la Chopin valse)

VAR. V (a la Schumann)

VAR. VI

VAR. VII (a la Polonaise)

Maestoso ♩ = c. 80

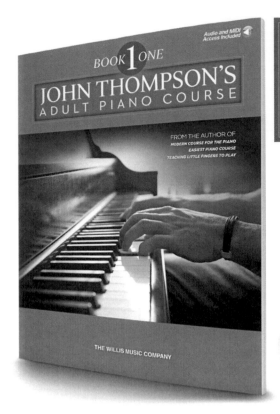

REDISCOVER
JOHN THOMPSON'S ADULT PIANO COURSE

ADULT PIANO COURSE

Recently re-engraved and updated, *John Thompson's Adult Piano Course* was compiled with the mature student in mind. Adults have the same musical road to travel as the younger student, but the study material for mature students will differ slightly in content. Since these beloved books were written and arranged especially for adults, they contain a wonderful mix of classical arrangements, well-known folk-tunes and outstanding originals that many will find a pleasure to learn and play. Most importantly, the student is always encouraged to play as artistically and with as much musical understanding as possible. Access to orchestrations online is available and features two tracks for each piece: a demo track with the piano part, and one with just the accompaniment.

00122297	Book 1 – Book/Online Audio	$14.99
00412639	Book 1 – Book Only	$6.99
00122300	Book 2 – Book/Online Audio	$14.99
00415763	Book 2 – Book Only	$6.99

POPULAR PIANO SOLOS – JOHN THOMPSON'S ADULT PIANO COURSE

12 great arrangements that can be used on their own, or as a supplement to *John Thompson's Adult Piano Course*.
Each book includes access to audio tracks online that be downloaded or streamed.

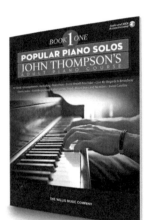

BOOK 1
arr. Carolyn Miller
Born Free • Can't Help Falling in Love • Every Breath You Take • Fields of Gold • Give My Regards to Broadway • A Groovy Kind of Love • My Life • Ob-La-Di, Ob-La-Da • Open Arms • Raindrops Keep Fallin' on My Head • Rainy Days and Mondays • Sweet Caroline.

00124215 Book/Online Audio $12.99

BOOK 2
arr. Eric Baumgartner & Glenda Austin
And So It Goes • Beauty and the Beast • Getting to Know You • Hey Jude • If My Friends Could See Me Now • Lollipop • My Favorite Things • Nadia's Theme • Strawberry Fields Forever • Sunrise, Sunset • Sway (Quien Será) • You Raise Me Up.

00124216 Book/Online Audio $12.99

Also Available, JOHN THOMPSON RECITAL SERIES:

SPIRITUALS
Intermediate to Advanced Level
Six excellent arrangements that are ideal for recital or church service. Titles: Deep River • Heav'n, Heav'n • I Want to Be Ready (Walk in Jerusalem, Jus' like John) • Nobody Knows De Trouble I've Seen • Short'nin' Bread • Swing Low, Sweet Chariot.

00137218 .... $6.99

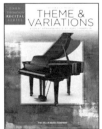

THEME AND VARIATIONS
Intermediate to Advanced Level
Fantastic recital variations that are sure to impress: Chopsticks • Variations on Mary Had a Little Lamb • Variations on Chopin's C Minor Prelude • Three Blind Mice - Variations on the Theme • Variations on Twinkle, Twinkle, Little Star.

00137219.............................. $8.99

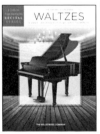

WALTZES
Intermediate to Advanced Level
Excellent, virtuosic arrangements of famous romantic waltzes: Artist's Life (Strauss) • Paraphrase on the Beautiful Blue Danube (Strauss) • Dark Eyes (Russian Cabaret Song) • Vienna Life (Strauss) • Waltz of the Flowers (Tchaikovsky) • Wedding of the Winds (John T. Hall).

00137220.............................. $8.99

Prices, contents, and availability subject to change without notice.